Disney's Year Book 1993

GROLIER ENTERPRISES INC.
Danbury, Connecticut

FERN L. MAMBERG	*Executive Editor*
MICHÈLE A. MCLEAN	*Art Director*
HARRIETT GREYSTONE	*Production Manager*

ISBN: 0-7172-8324-0
ISSN: 0273-1274

Illustration Credits and Acknowledgments

6—Artist, Michèle A. McLean; © Karl Gehring/Gamma-Liaison; © Ashe/Gamma Liaison; 7—© Linda L. Creighton/*U.S. News & World Report;* 8—© Ira Wyman/Sygma; 9—© James D. Wilson/Gamma-Liaison; 10–11—© Art Wolfe; 12—© Art Wolfe; 12–13—© Art Wolfe; 13—© Leonard Lee Rue/Animals Animals; © Joe McDonald/Animals Animals; 14—© Jane Burton/Bruce Coleman, Inc.; © Breck P. Kent/Animals Animals; 15—© Tim Davis/Photo Researchers, Inc.; 28–29—© Rick Friedman/Black Star; 29—© Peter Menzel; 30—© W. Campbell/ Sygma; © Tom & Pat Leeson/DRK Photos; 31—© G. Ziesler/ Peter Arnold, Inc.; 32–33—© Dwight Kuhn; 34–35—Artist, Ned Shaw; 48—© E. S. Ross; © William M. Partington/Photo Researchers, Inc.; © J. L. Castner; © E. S. Ross; 49—© E. S. Ross; © J. L. Castner; © Sturgis McKeever/Photo Researchers, Inc.; © E. S. Ross; 50—© Sipa Sport; © Richard Martin/Allsport; 51—© Rick Stewart/Allsport; 52—© George Tiedemann/*Sports Illustrated;* © Neil Leifer/Camera 5; 53—© David Madison/Duomo; 54—© Neil Leifer/Camera 5; 55—© William R. Sallaz/Duomo; © Duomo; 68—© Janis Miglavs/Image Source; 68–69—© Peter Thomann/*Stern;* 69–70—© Janis Miglavs/Image Source; 72–73—Buttons courtesy of Tender Buttons, New York City; 86—© Ken Highfill/Photo Researchers, Inc.; 87—© Stephen Krasemann/ DRK Photos; © Hans Pfletschinger/Peter Arnold, Inc.; 88—© E. Hanumantha Rao/Photo Researchers, Inc.; © C. Allan Morgan/Peter Arnold, Inc.; 89—© Patti Murray/Animals Animals; 90–91—Artist, Vince Caputo; 92–95—© Richard T. Nowitz

Contents

A NEW PRESIDENT FOR THE UNITED STATES

People in the United States voted in an important election in 1992. They chose a new president, Bill Clinton (left), and a new vice-president, Al Gore (right). Clinton and Gore were the candidates of the Democratic Party. The symbol of the Democrats is the donkey—that's why a donkey is holding the posters here.

Clinton and Gore defeated the Republican candidates, President George Bush and Vice-President Dan Quayle. (The Republicans have a symbol, too—the elephant.) Bush had been president since 1989. Before that, he had been vice-president for eight years, under President Ronald Reagan. So the 1992 election marked a big change for the United States. It was the first time a Democrat was elected president in twelve years.

Why did Americans vote for change? There were many reasons. But the main reason was the economy. Many people were out of work. Businesses weren't growing, and neither were family incomes. Clinton, who was governor of Arkansas at the time of the election, promised to do more to help solve these problems.

The outgoing team: President George Bush and First Lady Barbara Bush (right), and Vice-President Dan Quayle and his wife, Marilyn.

The new First Lady, Hillary Clinton, and First Daughter, Chelsea, have a new address: The White House, 1600 Pennsylvania Avenue.

The Democrats and the Republicans campaigned from early in the year until Election Day—November 3. They made speeches and appeared on television. Each candidate tried to convince the voters that he would do the best job. In the end, Clinton won 43 percent of the vote, while Bush won 38 percent.

But the 1992 election was unusual. In most years, the Republicans and Democrats get almost all the votes. However, in 1992, an independent candidate did very well. He was H. Ross Perot, a billionaire from Texas. Perot entered the race very late, on October 1, yet he won 19 percent of the vote.

After the long campaign and election, Clinton had time to rest. He would take office as president on Inauguration Day—January 20, 1993. But meanwhile, he had a lot of work to do, planning for the next four years.

Kids Voting USA

To vote in a U.S. election, you must be 18 years old. But in 1992, in eleven states, more than a million schoolchildren—some as young as 5—cast ballots. What was going on?

The children took part in a special program called "Kids Voting USA." With their parents' permission, they "registered" to vote just as adult voters do. In school, they talked about the candidates and issues. Then, on Election Day, they went to official polling places and cast special ballots. Their votes didn't count, but the children learned about voting. And the people who ran the program said that more adults turned out to vote in places that had the program!

"Kids Voting" ballots had a donkey (for Clinton) and an elephant (for Bush).

WHOOO GIVES A HOOT!

It's late at night, and a wood mouse is scurrying across the forest floor. Far above, on a pine branch, a hunter hears the soft patter of its feet. In an instant, the hunter swoops down and snatches the mouse in its powerful talons. Back on the branch, the hunter swallows its prey in one gulp. The hunter is an owl, a member of one of the most fascinating families of birds.

There are more than 130 kinds of owls in the world, with 20 of them in North America. They are found in every part of the world. Snowy owls are at home in the Arctic tundra. Burrowing owls inhabit grasslands. Elf owls live in deserts. Screech owls live in towns and cities. Woodland owls make their homes from the cool pine forests of the north to the tropical rain forests.

Owls also vary greatly in size. The smallest are the elf owl of the southwestern United States and the least pygmy owl of Central and South America. They are only about 5 inches long. The largest owls are the eagle owl of Europe, Asia, and northern Africa, and the great owl of Alaska and Canada. They measure about 30 inches.

Owls all have the same general shape: a large head with a hooked beak, no neck to speak of, and large feet with sharp claws. And since all owls are meat-eaters, they use their claws to grasp and hold a victim.

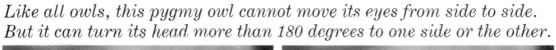

Like all owls, this pygmy owl cannot move its eyes from side to side. But it can turn its head more than 180 degrees to one side or the other.

Owls have huge eyes. They are much larger than those of other birds, and they help owls to see even in the dimmest light. In addition, the eyes are set to face forward (like your eyes) rather than to the side (like most birds'

Top: These great gray owlets will become the largest of owls. Center: Burrowing owls nest in underground tunnels. Left: The tiny elf owl lives in wood-pecker holes in cactus plants.

Above: Screech owls live in towns and cities and are the most common owls in North America. Left: The snowy owl makes its summer home (where it breeds) in the snow-covered Arctic tundra.

eyes). This allows an owl to judge distance when catching prey. But an owl cannot move its eyes from side to side. Instead, the owl turns its head.

Owls also have a remarkable sense of hearing. An owl's hearing is far more sensitive than human hearing. Many owls can tell with pinpoint accuracy where a sound is coming from. Thus they can hunt in almost total darkness. Owls need these super senses because most are nocturnal—they hunt for their food by night. And not all owls call "whooo, whooo." Many owl calls are strange, ranging from bone-chilling hoots to unearthly shrieks.

What's on the Menu?

Most owls' favorite foods are mice and other small rodents. And, like the barn owl pictured here, owls usually swallow their prey whole —fur, bones, and all. But an owl can't digest fur and bone. Instead, these materials are packed into pellets inside the owl's stomach. Every so often, the owl burps up a pellet, and it's dropped on the ground. Owl pellets look like fuzzy lumps. If you find one, you can take it apart to see what was on the owl's menu, as was done by a scientist in the picture below. First, soak the pellet in warm water, and then gently pull it apart with tweezers. You might find skulls, jaws, beaks, teeth, fur, and feathers.

An owl's skill as a hunter makes it valuable in controlling pests. A pair of barn owls can eat about 1,300 rats a year. Despite this helpful role, owls have often been hunted by people. And they are sometimes killed by pesticides. But the greatest danger facing many kinds of owls today is the destruction of their habitats.

Among those in danger are northern spotted owls, which live only in the forests of the Pacific Northwest. As more and more timber is taken from these forests, the owls have fewer places to live. Only a few thousand of these owls now remain. Environmentalists want logging to be stopped. But the timber industry says that logging is important to the area's economy.

The northern spotted owl is in danger of dying out.

In 1992, the U.S. government said that it would restrict logging in some forest areas of the Pacific Northwest. But it also said that the logging industry could cut down trees on about 1,700 acres of forests where northern spotted owls live. So at least for now, the future of this endangered owl remains uncertain.

THE TROUBLE WITH WISHES

Once upon a time there was a band of fairies who lived in an enchanted forest. During the day it looked like any other forest. But at night it was aglow with fairy magic.

Next to the forest was a kingdom with a castle and farms and fields.

The people in the kingdom and the fairies in the forest lived very peacefully together until one of the farmers decided to make his field larger. He chopped down some of the trees in the enchanted forest.

Of course the fairies were upset, so they cast all their best spells on the farmer.

The poor man woke up the next morning to find that his cow's milk was green. Who would drink it? The next day he found that his chickens were roosting upside down. How could they lay any eggs? And the following day his pigs refused to eat. What good was a skinny pig?

The farmer went straight to the King to tell him what had happened. The King went straight to the royal wizard. The wizard went straight to his book of magic.

"Ah-ha!" the wizard cried. "What we need is a giant, to scare away the fairies." He turned to the King. "Go hire a giant, Your Majesty," he suggested.

When the giant arrived, the King was up on a ladder fixing the drawbridge.

"Ho, ho, hum!" boomed the giant. "Where are all these fairies you hired me to frighten away?" The giant's voice was so loud that it shook the walls of the castle, and the King almost fell off his ladder.

"Over in the forest," the King replied.

The giant stomped off toward the forest, shaking the ground as he went. In about an hour, he stomped back to the castle and told the King that the fairies had fled.

"Thank you for your help," said the King. "You can be on your way now."

But the giant was in no hurry to leave. He liked the kingdom, and so he decided to stay. However, he caused more problems than he had solved. Whenever he walked, he squashed the crops. When he played marbles, he used huge

rocks that knocked down houses. And when he slept, his snores were so loud that he kept the whole village awake.

This time a dozen farmers went to see the King.

The King again went to the wizard, and the wizard again went to look in his book of magic.

"Ah-ha!" he said. "What you need is a dragon to scare away the giant. Go hire a dragon, Your Majesty."

And that very day the King hired a dragon.

When the dragon arrived, the King was standing on the castle wall looking at all the damage that the giant had caused during his stay.

"Hi, King," called the dragon as he curled himself around a tower. "Where's this giant who's been giving you trouble?" The dragon's flaming breath sent sparks to settle on the king's second-best shirt.

"Follow the snores," said the King, looking at the little black holes in his sleeve.

Well, the dragon scared the giant away, but he caused more trouble than the giant had. He liked the kingdom, too, especially one of the castle towers. He curled up around it and went to sleep. He snored even louder than the giant had. His fiery breath popped all the corn in the fields, scorched all the laundry that had been hung out to dry, and singed the wool on all the sheep.

This time every farmer in the kingdom went to see the King.

Once more, the King went to his wizard, and once more the wizard went to look in his book of magic.

"Ah-ha!" he cried. "What you need is a knight to scare away the dragon. Go hire a knight, Your Majesty."

It didn't take the knight long to scare the dragon away, but he too decided he liked the kingdom. However, he wasn't a very good guest.

23

He ate all the food in the castle. He refused to help out around the castle. And when he practiced his jousting, he used the farmers' scarecrows for targets. This made all the town children want to watch him instead of doing their chores. So tables weren't set for dinner, dishes went unwashed after meals, and beds didn't get made.

This time, all the farmers and all their wives went to see the King.

With a great big sigh, the King went to see the wizard,

and with an even bigger sigh, the wizard again opened his book of magic.

"Ah-ha!" he cried. "All you need to do is marry the knight off to the princess who lives in the next kingdom."

"But what if she doesn't like him?" asked the King

"Simple," replied the wizard. "We'll give them both a love potion."

"And where are we going to get a love potion?" asked the King.

"Why, from the fairies, of course," the wizard said.

The King gave the wizard a funny look.

"Oh," said the wizard as he understood. "We don't have any more fairies, do we?"

Little by little, all the people in the kingdom realized how foolish they had been to trade a small problem for a much bigger one.

"If only there were a way to turn back time so that none of this would have happened!" sighed the King.

The wizard perked up. "Now that's something I can do!" he offered.

So the wizard cast a spell that turned back the time, and everything was as it had been before. The farmer had never cut down the enchanted trees. The fairies had never cast their spells. The giant, the dragon, and the knight had never come to the kingdom. The King and his wizard, all the farmers and their wives and children, and even the fairies lived happily ever after. And no one ever, ever cut down another enchanted tree.

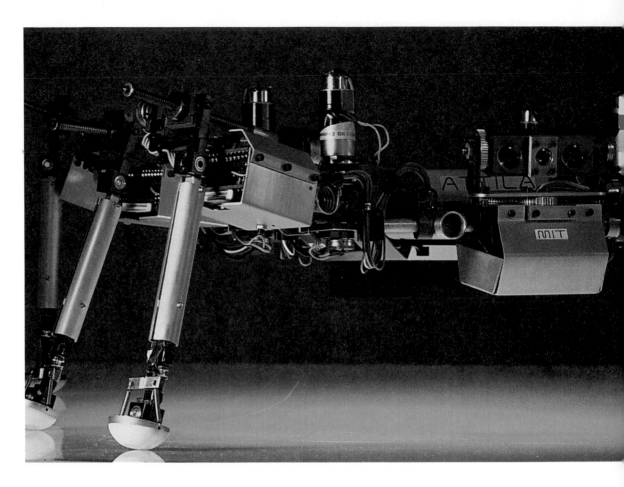

HERE COME THE BUGBOTS!

Attila the ant. Squirt the cockroach. The Nerd Herd. You won't run into these creatures in the woods. Their home is in a science lab—and they're not living things at all! They are small insectlike robots called "bugbots." The robot scientists who are developing them say that the bugbots will be faster, better, and less expensive than large robots.

Let's take a look at Attila. This bugbot is a little over a foot long and weighs three-and-a-half pounds. Packed into its body are 150 sensors that gather information about the environment.

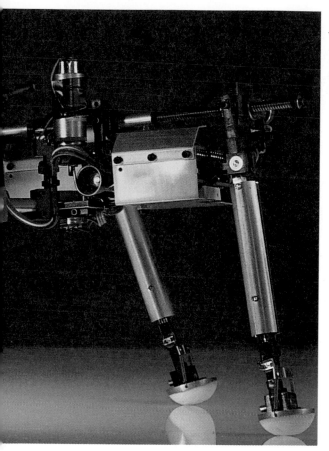

Attila—a fourteen-inch-long bugbot.

But when one of the scientists claps his hands, Squirt comes out of its hiding place to investigate.

Bugbots may someday play a role in space exploration. Attilas could be sent to Mars to send pictures back to Earth. Another plan calls for developing a group of robots named the Nerd Herd and sending them to the moon.

One day, bugbots might be a part of every home. You might even have a bugbot for a pet!

Attila has video-camera eyes, and range finders that help it judge distances. Other sensors tell it if an object is in the way or if the ground is soft or solid. Tiny computers inside Attila's body are programmed to respond to all this information.

Squirt the cockroach has been programmed to stay away from light, so it hides in dark places.

Using a magnifying lens, a scientist works on a tinier bugbot.

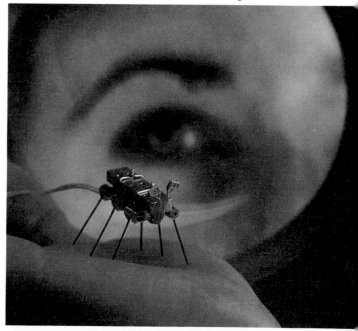

The disappearance of the world's forests can harm the environment.

THE VANISHING FOREST

Today, forests cover only a fraction of the land that they once did. Millions of acres have been destroyed. And those forests that remain are quickly disappearing. Their trees are being cut for timber or killed by pollution, or the land is being cleared for various uses. When the trees are gone, the plants and animals that once lived in the forest die out as well. And the loss of forests can have serious effects on the Earth's environment.

In many countries, forests are cut to create farmland or grazing land for cattle. In other places they are cleared for roads, housing developments, shopping centers, and factories. And in some areas timber companies say that if loggers lose their jobs, they will be unable to earn a living.

Environmentalists and others say that we must stop the destruction—and soon. People need to find ways to take products from forests without destroying them, and to use recycled paper and other materials rather than cutting trees. Our forests are too important to lose.

A margay cat in a Peruvian rain forest. When a forest is gone, its animals die out as well.

Ring Around the Tree

Did you know that if you come across the stump of a tree, you can tell its age? The tree's age is shown in a series of yearly growth rings. A complete growth ring has two bands. One is a band of light-colored wood formed in the spring. The other is a band of dark wood formed in the winter. Counting the rings tells you how old the tree was when it was cut.

When a tree dies naturally—from old age, wind damage, or fire—it can benefit the life of the forest. It returns nutrients to the soil. And it helps the growth of new plant and animal life. In this way, the forest recycles itself.

New maple leaves sprout from a log.

A family of mice live beneath a tree limb.

Fairy cups grow on a fallen tree.

A spotted salamander eats an earthworm.

Mushrooms grow among the foliage.

WHAT'S IN A COLOR?

Did you know that candy and other sweet foods seem to taste better when they come out of a pink box or are served on a pink plate? That wearing brown clothes can make people trust you more? That blue classroom walls have led to higher test scores?

The reasons why people choose certain colors can be very complicated. Colors can affect your behavior and your moods. They can even affect how other people react to you.

Some colors seem to bring about a response almost from birth. Babies react to the color red, for example, a few days after they are born. This attraction to red continues throughout life. But boys seem to like a fire-engine red. Girls tend to choose reds such as raspberry.

Pink seems to have a calming effect on people. In one study, prison convicts who became angry or upset were put in a bright pink room. They calmed down quickly. Blue also has a calming effect. Deep blue seems to send a message of strength and trust, and pale blue is said to bring on daydreaming. Yellow often has the opposite effect—it can make people nervous and anxious. Studies have shown that babies cry more in yellow rooms.

Color choices are very important for many businesses. The color scheme of a workplace can affect the way people work. And the color of a package on a supermarket shelf can affect sales. For example, experts say that laundry soap sells best in a blue and orange box.

Now that you know something about color, it may help you decide what color clothes you should wear!

Red seems to make people eat more and stay longer in restaurants.

Pink has a calming effect on people. Sweets from a pink box seem to taste better.

Splashes of yellow are cheery, but too much makes us jumpy.

Green makes people feel safe and secure—perhaps because most of nature is green.

Blue is most people's favorite color. It means authority and knowledge. And people eat less from blue plates.

THE PERFECT CRIME WAVE

Mickey and Goofy were sitting in Chief O'Hara's office.

"I don't understand it, Mickey!" the police chief said. "There's a crime wave going on, but we haven't caught any crooks!"

"Gawrsh!" Goofy gasped. "They must be pretty smart crooks!"

"That's what's so crazy, Goofy," the Chief said. "All the crimes in this crime wave have been, well . . . goofy."

The chief began to read from some reports. "Manhole covers, rubber baby-buggy bumpers, silk shoelaces all stolen!"

"Why would someone steal those things?" Mickey wondered.

"I don't know," the Chief said. "I need your help, Mickey!"

"My help, too, Chief?" Goofy asked.

Chief O'Hara shrugged. "Sure, Goofy."

"I'll get right on it, Chief!" Mickey promised. Then he and Goofy left the police station.

For the first time in his long crime-fighting career, Mickey was completely puzzled by a case.

"What would a crook want with rugger bubby . . . er, baggy bumpy . . . " Goofy tried to say as the two friends walked along.

"Rubber baby-buggy bumpers!" Mickey said, helping Goofy through the tongue-twister.

"Yeah. Those things," Goofy said.

"I don't have a clue," Mickey replied. "I don't even know where to begin. This crime wave is too goofy . . . if you'll pardon the word, Goofy. I guess you'd better take me home. I have a lot of thinking to do about this case."

Suddenly a figure stepped out of a dark alley and growled, "Stick 'em up!"

Mickey and Goofy stuck 'em up.

"Gimme me all your pots and pans!" he demanded.

Mickey couldn't believe it. "We don't have any pots and pans!"

"Drat!" snorted the disappointed crook. "Thanks, anyway." He ran back into the alley, jumped a fence, and was gone.

Mickey scratched his head. "Another crazy crime," he said.

"Wait a minute, Mick," said Goofy, running into the alley. When he came back, he was holding a newspaper. "That fellow must have dropped this when he jumped over the fence."

"Let me see it," said Mickey. He opened the paper. "I don't see any clues here," he reported. "It's just today's paper."

Goofy took the newspaper. "I haven't read the comics today," he said, rolling up the paper and putting it in his pocket.

As Goofy drove home he thought that he'd never seen Mickey feeling so low. "Poor Mickey," he said to himself.

"He's used to solving *smart* crimes. These *dumb* crimes have got him down."

When Goofy got home, he wondered if he should think about the case. But he wasn't much good at thinking. So he pulled the newspaper from his pocket and opened it to the comics.

It was then that something caught his eye. At the top of the comics page was Sidney Stargazer's horoscope column. Goofy had seen it a million times, but in this copy someone had made a red X in front of the horoscope for Taurus.

Here is what that horoscope said:

Taurus (April 20—May 20):
Focus on marital status, direction, obtaining pots and pans.

Pots and pans? Wasn't that what the crook had wanted? This was the crook's newspaper. Could this be a clue—one that Goofy had found and Mickey had missed?

Usually, when ideas knocked on the door of Goofy's brain, they didn't find Goofy at home. But today he was letting them in.

"Gawrsh!" Goofy thought. "Mickey and Chief O'Hara would sure be proud of me if *I* was the one who solved this case!"

Goofy thought carefully. What would Mickey do first?

Goofy ran outside, jumped in his car, and went to the newspaper office. "I gotta see Sidney Stargazer right away!" he said to the young woman at the front desk.

"Mr. Stargazer is on vacation," she told him. "Another astrologer is writing his column while he's gone."

"If the new guy wrote this," Goofy said, "I need to talk to him."

"He doesn't work here," she told him. "Here's his address."

Goofy took the slip of paper. "Thanks!" he said.

The address turned out to be an old warehouse. Over the door was a sign that read: "Professor Zodiac, Astrologer."

Goofy opened the door slowly, wishing Mickey were there, too. Inside the warehouse it was dark, except for a single light that burned at the far end of the big, messy floor. Under the lamp, two men were seated at a desk. They were so busy talking that they didn't see Goofy come in.

Goofy recognized one of the men! "Gawrsh!" he thought. "It's that fellow that tried to rob us!"

"But, Professor Zodiac," the robber was saying, "nobody carries pots and pans around. Tell me something else to steal!"

Professor Zodiac hit the desk with his fist. A stack of pots clattered. "Be quiet!" he boomed. "The rest of the gang have found pots and pans. I'm going to create the perfect crime wave! The stars tell me that today you have to steal pots and pans!"

Professor Zodiac stood up and pointed to the star chart on the

wall behind his desk. "Look! Saturn is in the eighth house," he explained. "If you try to steal anything but pots and pans today, you'll

get caught! My perfect crime wave will be spoiled!"

"Some crime wave!" the robber grumbled. He pointed to the piles of manhole covers, shoelaces, and baby-buggy bumpers all over the warehouse floor. "Look at this junk! When are we going to start stealing something useful—like money?"

"When the stars tell us to!" the Professor snapped. "Now, get out of here and bring me back some pots and pans! If I don't figure out tomorrow's horoscopes, I won't know what to tell any of the gang to steal tomorrow."

The crook turned to leave, and at that point fate played a dirty trick on Goofy. His newspaper plopped out of his pocket!

The crook turned toward the sound and discovered Goofy.

"Hey, Professor!" he called out. "Did the stars tell you that you were going to have a visitor today?"

"No," Professor Zodiac answered.

"Well, you have one," the crook said, ordering Goofy over to the desk.

Goofy approached the crook and the Professor, his hands up

over his head. Because he wasn't watching where he was going, he didn't see the chair in front of the desk.

"Whoops!" cried Goofy as he lost his balance and bumped into the crook. The crook fell into the desk, and he and the Professor and the desk went flying into a jumble of manhole covers, shoelaces, and baby-buggy bumpers.

The mountain of junk wobbled for a moment. Then all the manhole covers, shoelaces, and baby-buggy bumpers came crashing down over the Professor and the crook and knocked them out cold! The crime wave was finally over.

"Gawrsh, I guess I'd better call the police," Goofy said. And

that's just what he did. A nice, strong police officer came to the warehouse and took the Professor and the crook off to jail.

Later, back at the police station, Mickey and Goofy once again sat with Chief O'Hara. "Well, Goofy," the Chief began, looking surprised, "thank you for solving the crime wave!"

"Aw, shucks," said Goofy. "I owe it all to them rugger buggy, er, baggy bumpy . . ."

"Rubber baby-buggy bumpers," Mickey chuckled. "Nope. We owe it all to you. Who else but Goofy could have solved the goofiest crime wave in the history of this city?"

Look for yellow spots in order to match this anise swallowtail with its caterpillar. Swallowtails are named for the tail-like projections on their hind wings.

When the gulf fritillary's caterpillar turned into an adult butterfly, its orange color became very bright. But it lost the long rows of black spines that protected the caterpillar against its enemies.

BABY PICTURES

When a butterfly is born, it doesn't look like a butterfly. It looks like a worm with lots of stumpy little legs. This is the caterpillar stage. When the caterpillar reaches its full size, its

Big bright "eyespots" on its wings make the buckeye butterfly look like a two-headed monster to hungry birds. The buckeye's caterpillar doesn't have eyespots. But its dark body is protected with spines.

Look at this zebra longwing and you'll see how this butterfly got its name! But there are no yellow stripes on the caterpillar. Instead, it looks like it's coated with icing.

body completely changes—it turns into a butterfly. Look at the "baby pictures" below. Can you guess which caterpillars turned into which butterflies above? The information next to each butterfly picture will give you clues.

ANSWERS: The anise swallowtail is caterpillar D; gulf fritillary, C; buckeye, B; zebra longwing, A.

C

D

Magique, the Winter Games mascot

GOING FOR THE GOLD

The 1992 Olympic Games brought together athletes from all over the world to compete for medals. Athletes from 63 countries tried for the gold at the 16th Winter Games, held in Albertville, France. And athletes from 172 countries competed at the 25th Summer Games, held in Barcelona, Spain. More than 300 gold medals were awarded. The shining performances of a few of the winners are described here.

Kristi Yamaguchi, U.S., figure skating

• It was a duel on ice for Kristi Yamaguchi of the United States when she won the women's figure-skating title at the Winter Games. She competed against some of the world's best skaters, including Midori Ito of Japan. But Yamaguchi's grace, speed, and stunning jumps earned her the gold. Even before the Olympics, Yamaguchi was number one. In March 1991 she had won her first world figure-skating title, and in January 1992, her first U.S. championship.

Toni Nieminen, Finland, ski jumping

• Toni Nieminen of Finland soared to fame when he captured three ski-jumping medals in his first ever Winter Olympics. In fact, it was the first time he had competed in any international competition. Nieminen won the gold medal in the large hill (120-meter) jump. He also won the bronze medal in the normal hill (90-meter) jump. And Nieminen was one of the Finnish jumpers whose combined talents won the gold medal in the 120-meter team event.

The "Flying Finn," who was a gymnast before he took up ski jumping, also leaped into the record books. At 16 years of age, he was the youngest male gold medalist in the entire history of the Winter Games.

• Jackie Joyner-Kersee of the United States proved once again that she was the world's greatest woman athlete when she won

Jackie Joyner-Kersee, U.S., seven-event heptathlon

Carl Lewis, U.S., long jump

the seven-event heptathlon at the Summer Games. It was her second straight Olympic heptathlon championship. The events in this difficult, two-day competition are the 100-meter hurdles, high jump, long jump, javelin, shot put, 200-meter race, and 800-meter race. (She is shown in the photo above clearing the high jump bar.) Joyner-Kersee also won the bronze medal in the individual long jump event at the Games.

• For the third Summer Olympics in a row, U.S. long jumper and sprinter Carl Lewis made the track and field competition a showcase for his talents. With a leap of 28 feet, 5½ inches, "King Carl" soared to his third straight Olympic long jump gold medal. In doing so, he topped teammate Mike Powell, the world record holder in the event. Lewis also anchored the U.S. 400-meter relay team, which raced to the gold in world record time. With that win, Lewis claimed his second gold medal of the 1992 Games, and the eighth of his Olympic career.

Fu Mingxia, China, diving

• Fu Mingxia of China won the gold medal in women's platform diving. At age 13, she was the youngest medalist of the 1992 Summer and Winter Games. Winning wasn't new to Mingxia. She started diving when she was 8—even before she could swim— and won the 10-meter world diving championship when she was 12.

• Vitaly Scherbo of the Unified Team was the outstanding performer in men's gymnastics at the Summer Games. He won six gold medals, including the individual all-around. The most golds won by any other athlete at the Games was three. In addition to winning the all-around, Scherbo won individual golds for his performances on the parallel bars, rings, vault, and pommel horse (which he tied with a North Korean gymnast). And he was a member of the Unified Team that defeated China and Japan for the team gold. (The Unified Team was made up of athletes from five former republics of the Soviet Union: Russia, Ukraine, Belarus, Kazakhstan, and Uzbekistan. Vitaly Scherbo is from Ukraine.)

Vitaly Scherbo, Unified Team, gymnastics

• The U.S. "Dream Team" captured the gold medal in basketball. This was no surprise, because the squad consisted of the best basketball players in the world. It included such pros as Earvin "Magic" Johnson, Michael Jordan, Larry Bird, and Patrick Ewing. Every game was a big win for the team, and some people complained about the lack of fairness. But professional athletes have been allowed to compete in the Olympics for some time. So such a great team was bound to appear. The gold medal game was a 117–85 defeat of Croatia (formerly a republic of Yugoslavia).

Although Magic Johnson was only tenth in scoring, he was one of the superstars of the

Magic Johnson of the U.S. "Dream Team," basketball

Olympics. No matter where he went, he attracted crowds. Because of his work on behalf of the fight against AIDS, many consider Magic Johnson to be a hero off the court as well as on.

The 1992 Winter and Summer Olympic Games were among the most exciting ever. And they made people hope that perhaps peace among nations of the world might well begin in the arena of international sport.

Cobi, the Summer Games mascot

The Seven Dwarfs to the Rescue

The Seven Dwarfs were rushing around their cottage, hurrying to get ready to go to lunch at Snow White's castle. Each dwarf was trying hard to look his best.

Sleepy wanted to be wide awake, so he splashed cold water on his face. Sneezy helped Bashful put his hat on just right. Happy was whistling as he shined his shoes, and Dopey was putting his belt on over a nice, clean robe. Grumpy was combing his beard in front of the mirror.

Doc was polishing his glasses when he came up with an idea. "Misten, len . . . er . . . listen, men," he said. "I think we should bring Snow White a gift, to thank her for inviting us to lunch."

"Achoo! Good idea," agreed Sneezy. "But what . . . achoo! . . . should we give her?"

"How about a bouquet of flowers?" Happy suggested. "Dopey and I will go pick some."

All the dwarfs agreed that flowers would make a perfect thank-you present, so Happy and Dopey went off into the woods to pick a bouquet.

"Don't take too long," Doc called after them. "We don't want to make Snow White worry because we're late."

The two dwarfs went straight to the pond where Happy had seen some flowers just yesterday. But they didn't find any.

"I know, Dopey," said Happy, pointing to the stream that ran into the pond and out again. "You go that way, upstream, and I'll go the other way, downstream."

Off Dopey went, looking for flowers. As he was walking along, he came upon a fallen log. He was about to climb over it when he saw a scared-looking bunny. Its foot was caught under the log.

Dopey tried to push the log off the bunny's foot, but he wasn't

strong enough. He would have gone back to get Happy to help him, but the rabbit looked so sad and lonely. What should he do?

In the meantime, Happy hadn't found any flowers. He decided to go back and see if Dopey had had any better luck.

Soon Happy came upon Dopey and the trapped bunny. Right away, the two dwarfs tried to lift the log to help the poor animal. But even with both dwarfs' strength, the log was too heavy to move.

"You stay here and keep the bunny company," Happy said to Dopey. "I'll go get the others."

Pretty soon Dopey heard the other dwarfs coming. As they marched along, they were singing, "Hi-ho, hi-ho, it's off to help we go!"

The silent little dwarf gave the bunny a gentle pat, to let it know that everything would be all right.

Meanwhile, as Doc had feared, Snow White was beginning to worry. "They promised they'd be here at noon," she said to herself. "They're awfully late. I'd better ask the Magic Mirror. It will tell me if anything's wrong."

Snow White went to the mirror and asked,

> *Mirror, mirror, help me see.*
>
> *Tell me where the dwarfs may be.*

The ghostly face appeared in the mirror and answered,

> *Wonder no more where the dwarfs may be.*
>
> *They're saving a bunny trapped under a tree.*

"Oh, dear!" cried Snow White. "I'd better go help them!"

As Snow White was hurrying to the forest, the Seven Dwarfs agreed on a plan to help the bunny. Sneezy, Grumpy, and Sleepy tied ropes around the log. They tossed the free ends of the ropes over a tree limb, grabbed the ends, and got ready to pull.

Bashful, Happy, and Doc were on the other side of the log, ready
to lift. When they were all in place, Happy gave the signal.

As the others pushed and pulled with all their might, Dopey
pulled the bunny out from under the log!

But although they expected the rabbit to hop away, it couldn't
do much more than stumble.

"Poor bunny!" said Doc. "We'd better take it back to the
cottage. We can't leave it here if it's hurt."

"You know, we're already late for lunch with Snow White,"
Grumpy grumbled. "This will only make us later."

"It can't be helped," said Doc. "We have to help this bunny.
Snow White will understand."

"Uh . . . she's a princess," Bashful pointed out. "It's not polite
to keep a princess waiting."

"We'll just have to hurry," said Happy.

As they neared the cottage, they saw Snow White coming in
her carriage.

"Look! Achoo! Someone's here," said Sneezy.

"It's Snow White! I bet she came to tell us off," said Grumpy.

"Well," said Doc, "we'll just have to face her."

But Snow White wasn't angry at all. "I was a little worried," she told them, "but the Mirror told me what had happened. Is this the little bunny who's hurt?"

"That's right," said Doc, picking up the bunny and handing it to Snow White. "It can't hop."

"Well, let's go inside and see what's wrong," Snow White suggested, tenderly cradling the rabbit.

They all trooped in the door behind the princess and crowded around her when she sat down by the hearth. The bunny lay quietly in her lap as she gently inspected its hurt foot.

"It's not broken," she announced, "but the foot needs to stay

clean, so you can't let the bunny try to hop around for a few days.
Can you find me something to use as a bandage?"

The dwarfs searched the cottage high and low, but since Snow
White had gone off to marry the prince and live in the castle,
they had put off doing the laundry. They couldn't find anything
clean that would also make a good bandage.

Turning back to Snow White, they all held up empty hands.

64

She smiled at her friends. "Don't worry," she told them. "We'll think of something." Then she felt a tug at her skirt. It was Dopey.

"What is it, Dopey?" she asked.

The silent little dwarf hesitated, then held up the hem of Snow White's skirt.

"What . . . " she wondered. Then she got it. "You're right, Dopey," she said. "My skirt is nice and clean. We can use a piece of it as a bandage." And she proceeded to tear off a strip of cloth.

Soon the rabbit's foot was bandaged. "There!" she said. "Now if you can just keep this bunny quiet for a few days . . . "

"But, Princess," said Doc, "we can't stay home to watch him. We have to work."

"Well," said Snow White, standing up with the rabbit in her arms, "then we'll just take him to the castle." She walked to the door. "Besides, you must all be hungry. I know I am."

"But, Princess," Doc protested, "we can't have lunch with you now." He looked down at his shirt, which was covered with leaves and bark from pushing the log. "We're all doo tirty . . . er . . . too dirty."

"And we were going to bring you a present," Happy added.

"That's silly," Snow White answered. "I don't need a present. Just having you there is what I care about. And it doesn't matter if your clothes are a little smudged." Then she smiled. "But you will have to wash your hands."

Snow White's carriage couldn't carry everyone, so the princess walked back to the castle with her seven good friends. Dopey pushed the little bunny in his wheelbarrow. And as they walked through the forest, they sang, "Hi-ho, hi-ho! It's off to lunch we go!"

Return of the **BOOMERANG**

VCR's. Compact discs. Computer games. The hi-tech gadgets we have today are amazing. But do you ever yearn for a simpler form of entertainment. Well, what could be simpler than tossing a piece of wood as far as you can and then watching it sail right back at you? This round-trip object is a curved stick called a boomerang. When you learn to throw it correctly, you can play catch with yourself all day long.

It's believed that "rangs" were first invented about 11,000 years ago by the aborigines of Australia. They probably used

with a gradual, smooth curve at the point where the two arms meet. Each of the arms, which are also called blades, looks like an airplane wing—flat on the bottom and curved on top. But this basic shape can have many variations. There are rangs with three, four, and

Thrown correctly, a boomerang will make a round-trip flight.

the objects for hunting. Today, boomerangs have become popular for both sport and play.

What is the "right" shape for a boomerang? We usually picture a boomerang as being in the form of a wide V

Boomerang lessons: Grip one of the arms and throw directly overhand.

even six arms! Still other rangs are shaped like triangles. And
some are shaped like the letters H, S, or T.

How does a boomerang work? Because the arms of a
boomerang are shaped like airplane wings, a boomerang produces
the same sort of lifting force that an airplane's wings do. The
rang, like a plane, will rise in the direction of the curved side.
This is why a well-thrown boomerang seems to sail. But the
boomerang is spinning at the same time, the arms creating a
circle as it flies. The boomerang's lift, the speed of its forward
motion, and the spin of its arms all combine to cause the
boomerang to turn and come back.

Learning to throw a rang so that it returns takes practice.

Making a Boomerang

Make this simple boomerang, to use in a gym. Start with a piece of stiff cardboard at least 8 inches wide. With ruler and compass, draw the boomerang. The small center circle should be about 1½ inches in diameter. The larger circle is about 3¼ inches in diameter. Measuring from the edge of the large circle, draw each arm of the boomerang about 3 inches long. The arms gradually increase in width. Now cut out the boomerang, including the center circle.

Begin with the proper grip. Hold the boomerang with your thumb and fingers wrapped around the end of one arm. The "V" point is placed over your shoulder. The curved side of the arm is toward you, and the flat side is away from you.

The key to tossing a rang correctly is to throw overhand—directly overhand, as close to the vertical as possible. Pitch the boomerang toward the horizon, and snap your wrist as you release it. This snap is important—it helps create the spin that makes the rang fly. Once you've learned the technique, you'll be set for hours of fun. (Just one word of caution: Practice in a broad, open field—NEVER throw a boomerang near people or buildings.)

WHO'S GOT THE BUTTON?

Buttons are common objects that make getting dressed much easier. But buttons aren't just useful. You can collect them, play games with them, or use them to make jewelry.

People have collected buttons for a very long time. You can start your own collection today. Just ask your mother or grandmother to let you look through their button boxes. Later, you might want to buy buttons at flea markets or button shops.

You can keep your buttons in many kinds of containers—glass candy jars, wooden boxes, and clear plastic boxes. Don't use metal containers, though. They can rust, and this will damage any metal buttons you might have.

If you would like to use your buttons to create jewelry, here's a simple necklace that you can make. All you need is a strong piece of thread and lots of pretty buttons. They should be about the same size.

Using a sewing needle, thread on the buttons. If you don't have enough buttons for a necklace, you can sew small circles of felt between each button. When the necklace is long enough, just tie both ends of the thread together and slip your button necklace over your head. If you would like to try something a little more difficult, see if you can create a button doll like the one shown here.

Fanciful Fasteners

Among the most fascinating —and fun—buttons to collect are those that don't look like buttons at all! They're shaped like animals, flowers, and foods . . . pencils and hearts . . . letters and numbers . . . musical notes and planets. In fact, buttons come in almost every shape you can think of!

The Ghost City Under The Sea

One morning Ariel and Flounder met Ariel's sister Attina, who had her nose buried in a book.

"Ouch! Watch where you're swimming!" Attina complained.

"Sorry," Ariel apologized, glancing at the book's title. "*Ghost Towns Under the Sea*," she read. "Are there really such things?"

"Sure," Attina said. "There's even a human ghost city in the Eastern Ocean."

"Oh, Flounder," sighed Ariel, "I wish I could go to that human ghost city! I bet there are millions of neat things there."

"Forget it," Flounder said. "Your father would never let you. Besides, there are probably ghosts in a ghost city!"

As Ariel and Flounder spoke, two eels were watching. They slithered away to report to their mistress, Ursula the Sea Witch.

"Wonderful, my pets," Ursula crooned, stroking Flotsam and Jetsam. "If Ariel wants to see the human ghost city under the Eastern Ocean, I'll arrange it! But she'll be sorry!"

The next day, a messenger came to Triton's palace and invited
Ariel to sing her first solo at a concert in the Eastern Ocean. The
concert would be held in three days.

Triton was proud of his youngest daughter. But he wouldn't let
her go.

"Why not, Daddy?" Ariel exclaimed.

"I can't go with you, and it's too dangerous for you to travel
that far by yourself," Triton explained.

"Your Majesty," said Sebastian, "I can go with her."

"Good idea," Triton replied. "Why didn't I think of that?"

"We must leave right away," said the messenger.

Ariel, Sebastian, and Flounder, who refused to be left behind,
swam quickly after the messenger.

When they arrived in the Eastern Ocean, the messenger told them to wait. Then he disappeared.

"Now where did that messenger go?" Sebastian wondered. "I'll have a look around. You two, don't move a fin!" he added.

While they were waiting, Ariel saw a light flickering near some strange-looking hills. "Let's go see what's over there," she suggested. "Maybe it's the human ghost city."

Flounder didn't want to, but he followed Ariel. Suddenly the little mermaid came face to face with a terrible monster. It had sharp teeth, a long tail, and wicked-looking eyes.

It took Ariel a moment to realize that the "monster" was only a

picture on a stone wall. She swam past it into a beautiful room.

As Flounder hurried after her, Ariel picked up a small yellow bowl with a funny handle.

"Look, Flounder," Ariel said as she examined the odd yellow bowl. "It has a picture of that monster on it."

"Let's get out of here!" Flounder urged. "This place is giving me the creeps!"

"Okay, but I'm going to take this pretty little bowl along to put in my treasure room," Ariel decided.

Suddenly the beast from the picture came to life and leaped off the wall. It headed straight for Ariel!

"Swim, Flounder!" Ariel shouted, dropping the yellow bowl.

Ariel could feel the beast's hot breath on her tail. Suddenly,

they reached another wall. They turned to face the monster.

Pressing against the wall, Ariel accidentally touched a secret spring. A door opened in the wall and let them into another room. Then it closed right in the monster's face. The creature began beating on the stone wall.

Ariel looked around the room. For a moment she forgot the danger nearby.

"Oh, Flounder!" Ariel exclaimed. "Just look at all these beautiful human things!"

"Come on, Ariel!" Flounder shouted. "The monster's gonna break down the wall!"

They quickly found a way out and raced away. As they left the human ghost city, they bumped into Sebastian.

"Ariel, where have you been?" Sebastian scolded.

"I'm so sorry, Sebastian, but . . . " Ariel began to explain.

"Never mind, child," Sebastian said. "This is my new friend, Tyrus the sea turtle. He told me that someone must have been

playing a practical joke on us. There is no concert. In fact, Tyrus says there's no kingdom here anymore, only that old human ghost town over there."

"Yes," Tyrus put in. "It was buried by an earthquake."

"The earthquake must have buried the monster, too," Flounder said.

"What monster?" asked Tyrus.

"It was chasing us," Ariel explained.

"And it tried to eat us up," Flounder continued.

Suddenly there was a loud rumble, and the water around them began to swirl.

"Earthquake! " shouted Tyrus, pulling himself into his shell. "Swim for cover!"

Flounder swam as fast as he could, with Sebastian clinging to his tail. They both thought that Ariel was right behind them.

But the little mermaid was going back for the little golden bowl. Just as Ariel reached the ghost city, the monster burst through the wall and lunged at her.

Then the ocean floor opened up and the ghost city cracked apart, crashing down, down. A whirlpool rose from the hole in the ocean floor, catching the monster's tail. The beast was sucked into the whirlpool and vanished.

82

Ariel turned and swam after Sebastian and Flounder as fast as she could.

When they were all safe, Sebastian didn't have the heart to scold Ariel for her carelessness. "Let's go home," he said.

"Oh, Sebastian," Ariel said, "if we tell Daddy what happened, he won't ever let me go anywhere again. Unless, of course, we don't tell him exactly what happened . . . " she added. She hoped that Sebastian would keep their adventure a secret.

"We'll see, child," Sebastian said kindly. "You know I cannot lie to your father, and neither should you!"

Ariel nodded sadly.

When they got back, Ariel's
father and sisters welcomed
them.

King Triton turned to Sebastian
and asked proudly, "How did it
go, Royal Conductor?" Ariel held
her breath, waiting for Sebastian
to answer.

"Your Majesty, it was a smashing experience," Sebastian
responded. "But too far to travel," he added. "From now on, we
will stay closer to home."

"A wise choice, Sebastian," Triton agreed. "We missed you both far too much!"

Later, Ariel went to her treasure grotto. "I wish I could have saved some things from the human ghost city," she sighed.

"How about this?" Flounder said, pushing a round gold object toward Ariel.

"Oh, Flounder how did you get the bowl?" Ariel picked it up delightedly. Then she hugged him so tight that he squirmed.

"Aw, it was no big deal," Flounder said, blushing. "I saw it floating around after the earthquake. I wanted to surprise you."

"You're the best friend a mermaid could ever have," Ariel said, and she hugged Flounder again. This time, he didn't even wiggle!

A gray squirrel takes a snooze in a leaf nest perched high in the treetops.

ANIMAL HOMES

An airy leaf nest high atop a tree. A cozy underground burrow. A little pottery-jug nest against the side of a cliff. A termite nest that rises like a skyscraper into the sky. These are just a few of the many kinds of homes built by animals. Why do animals build homes? For the same reasons people do—so that they and their young will have shelter and protection.

Animal home-builders are different from human ones in a special way. People have to learn how to build homes. But animals inherit their building skills from their parents. Guided by instinct, an animal builds the right home the first time it tries.

Mammals are especially good home-builders. Some, like the gray squirrel, even have two homes. In winter, it lives in a tree hole, where it sleeps on a mattress of bark and leaves. In spring, it moves outside and builds a leaf nest high above the ground.

Mice, wolves, foxes, and other mammals live part of the time in underground burrows. The kit fox, for example, uses a burrow as a temporary nursery den. When the pups grow up, the den is abandoned.

Some of the most interesting homes are built by newly hatched insect

The underground burrow is the most popular type of home used by small mammals. This kit fox (above) uses it as a nursery den. Caddis worms (left) have fascinating underwater homes. They build case-like structures out of pebbles, wood, pine needles, or stone.

larvae called caddis worms. Caddis worms hatch from eggs laid in mountain ponds and streams. As soon as they wriggle out of their eggs, they begin to build case-like dwellings where they live until they leave the water as adult caddis flies. The cases are built out of wood, pebbles, pine needles, or stone.

Some people think that birds sleep in their nests. A few birds, such as owls and woodpeckers, actually do live in their nests. But most birds live in the open. They build nests only during the breeding season and use them as a sheltered cradle for their eggs and young.

The African weaver bird (left) builds a grass nest that dangles from a tree branch. Cliff swallows (below) build their nests, which look like little pottery jugs, beneath ledges to keep out the rain.

The African weaver bird lives in the tropics. It builds a covered nest that hangs by a loop from the branch of a tree. The nest may contain more than 300 strands of grass woven tightly into a ball. Inside the nest, the weaver bird hollows out a nesting chamber.

Cliff swallows build nests of mud mixed with their own sticky saliva. They smear the mud against the face of a cliff or the wall of a building and shape it into a little pottery jug with an opening at the top. The inside is lined with grass, moss, and feathers to cushion the eggs.

The African termite builds a towering mound that rises high into the air like a skyscraper.

Very few insects build nests. But they construct some of the architectural wonders of the animal world. African termites, for example, build towering skyscrapers that may rise 20 feet into the air. They are made out of soil that the termites chew and mix with their saliva—and the walls are as hard as concrete. Some termite mounds look like giant towers or mountain peaks.

A PEEK INTO THE FUTURE

The 21st century is quickly approaching. And it seems that everyone wants to know what the future will bring. How will people live and work? What sort of food will we eat? What kinds of cars will we drive? Will people find solutions to some of our many environmental problems? Here are a few predictions about the future.

Driving in the Next Century

The car of the future may be powered by electricity. Electric cars, which get their power from batteries, produce much less pollution than gasoline-powered cars. Electric models that are being built right now can travel 120 miles before their batteries have to be recharged. Cars of the future may also have electronic dashboard maps, and a joystick instead of a steering wheel.

Nutritious Recycling

People are finding some interesting ways to save our resources. For example, instead of plastic-foam or paper containers, fast-food restaurants of the future may serve food in packages you can eat! Some edible plates are already being made out of oatmeal and cornstarch. They aren't very tasty—but if you throw the plates away, they may provide food for wildlife.

Food From Outer Space

In the future, food will be grown in new ways. In a technique called hydroponics, vegetables are grown in a water solution instead of in soil. The plants are placed in an enclosed chamber. They aren't affected by the weather, and they can be grown year-round. Today it's expensive to grow foods this way. But huge hydroponic "farms" could be set up in space, on orbiting space stations. Then you could enjoy fresh vegetables that were truly out of this world!

Play astronaut at the controls of a spacecraft at Space Camp.

BLAST OFF TO SPACE CAMP

Have you ever wondered what it feels like to float weightless in space? To blast off in a rocket? To walk on the moon? To land on Mars? To bring the space shuttle to a perfect landing?

Most people can only read about space travel and follow astronauts' missions on television. But every year, thousands of young people can experience these things, and more, at U.S. Space Camp. They learn about space exploration by taking part in some of the training activities that are used by the U.S. astronauts.

There are actually two Space Camps in the United States. One is at the Alabama Space and Rocket Center in Huntsville, Alabama—the largest space museum in the world. The other is at the U.S. Astronaut Hall of Fame in Titusville, Florida, near the Kennedy Space Center. The camps accept students who are in grades 4 through 7. Campers come from all parts of the United States and from many other countries around the world. More than 130,000 people have attended. In fact, the camps have become so popular that similar camps have opened in Belgium and Japan. Others are planned for Spain, Canada, and Italy.

Each week at Space Camp is filled with excitement, discovery, and fun. Campers learn about the science and history of the U.S. space program. They find out how the space shuttle operates. They learn leadership skills and teamwork. And they have a great time while doing this. Here are some of the events campers can look forward to at Space Camp.

Tumble and spin in the Multi-Axis Trainer. This device is used by trainees to practice what to do when a spacecraft goes out of control.

Would you like to feel as if you're walking on the moon? You can, in the Microgravity Chair.

• **Rocket Building.** With computer instruction, campers learn how rockets are designed, propelled, and guided. They even build model rockets of their own and launch them, with a passenger— usually a cricket— aboard.

• **Astronaut Training.** Campers get to handle and try on the space suits and helmets used by astronauts. They taste the packaged foods that astronauts eat in space. And they examine and try out the systems that make space travel possible. These include the systems that get rid of wastes and that keep the astronauts safe and comfortable. Campers can also spin and tumble in the Multi-Axis Trainer, which acts like a spacecraft that's out of control.

• **Moon-Walking.** On the moon, an astronaut's weight is one sixth his or her weight on Earth. At Space Camp, campers get to use a Microgravity Chair, or moon-walk trainer. This device hangs from springs and reduces body weight to "moon weight." This gives the camper the sensation of walking on the moon.

• **Mars Mission.** NASA (the National Aeronautics and Space Administration) is planning the first manned mission to Mars. So campers take part in a simulated (make-believe) flight from Earth to Mars—with a stopover at a space station.

• **Space Shuttle Mission.** The high point of the week-long Space Camp is the simulated space shuttle flight. Campers go through all the steps of a shuttle mission: checkout, countdown, launch, orbit, and return to Earth.

• **Graduating.** Camp ends with a wonderful ceremony. All the campers receive space-camp wings, a certificate, and a group photo of their "astronaut" team— souvenirs of their thrilling adventure in "outer space."

In this Manned Maneuvering Unit, student astronauts can "take a walk in space."